GOVERNMENT OF CANADA

Rights and Responsibilities of Canadian Citizens

Edited by Heather C. Hudak

Weigl

Published by Weigl Educational Publishers Limited
6325 10th Street S.E.
Calgary, AB T2H 2Z9
Website: www.weigl.com

Library and Archives Canada Cataloguing-in-Publication Data available upon request.
Fax (403) 233-7769 WEIGL for the attention of the Publishing Records department.

ISBN 978-1-55388-680-8 (hard cover)
ISBN 978-1-55388-684-6 (soft cover)

Printed in the United States of America in North Mankato, Minnesota
1 2 3 4 5 6 7 8 9 0 14 13 12 11 10

082010
WEP230610

Project Coordinator: Heather C. Hudak
Project Editor: Brian Fitzgerald
Photo Research: Edward A. Thomas
Design: Tammy West

Weigl acknowledges Getty Images as its primary image supplier for this title.

We gratefully acknowledge the financial support of the Government of Canada
through the Canada Book Fund for our publishing activities.

CONTENTS

Introduction to Canada's Government

Large groups of people need rules for each member to follow. Most countries, cities, and towns have a government for this purpose. Government also organizes large groups of people to accomplish things an individual could not do alone. Most governments, for example, make and enforce laws, collect taxes, construct roads and bridges, educate children, and provide for defence.

Many countries, such as Canada, have a democratic form of government. The words *democratic* and *democracy* come from the Greek words *demos*, or "people," and *kratos*, or "power." In other words, the people have power.

There are two forms of democracy: **direct democracy** and **representative democracy**. Direct democracy gives every citizen the right to vote on every issue. Athens and many other city-states in ancient Greece governed themselves in this way. Requiring citizens across a large country to gather, debate ideas, and vote on every issue is not practical, however.

Most democratic countries, including Canada, are representative democracies. Citizens elect representatives to attend meetings, vote on issues, and make laws for them. Each person has a voice in government by voting in elections. However, only a small group of representatives has the power to make decisions.

Canada has three levels of government. Each level of government has its own powers and responsibilities. The federal government controls matters common to all provinces and territories. Provincial and territorial governments handle matters that are unique to each province and territory. Municipal governments manage matters that affect individual cities, towns, villages, and other municipalities.

People in a democratic society have the freedom to express their national pride.

Think about it!

1. List three things your government does that you could not do alone.

2. Why do you think Canada is a representative rather than a direct democracy?

3. Can you think of some advantages and disadvantages of having a representative government?

What is a Canadian Citizen?

A Canadian citizen is a person who either has been born in Canada or has sworn the **oath** of Canadian **citizenship** in front of a citizenship judge. In most cases, once a person becomes a Canadian citizen, he or she remains one for life.

Each citizen shares Canada's laws, traditions, and beliefs with his or her fellow citizens. All Canadian citizens have equal **rights**. A right is a freedom that is protected by law. Citizens have the freedoms of thought, speech, and religion, and they have the right to assemble in public. They also enjoy the right to enter, remain in, or leave Canada. They have the right to work and live in any province or territory they choose, as well as the right to carry a Canadian passport. Canadians who are at least 18 years old have the right to vote and to be a candidate in federal, provincial, and municipal elections.

All Canadians share the same rights and responsibilities.

Citizens have the same rights in all parts of Canada, including the most recently created territory, Nunavut.

Canadian citizens also have several important **responsibilities**, or duties. They must be loyal to their country, to the queen, and to the queen's main representative in Canada, the **governor general**. Canadian citizens must obey Canada's laws, care for the country's **heritage**, and support its ideals. The rights and responsibilities of citizens often go hand in hand. For example, all Canadians have the right to freely speak their mind. They also have a responsibility to respect the free speech of others.

All Canadian children have the right to a free education.

Defining Citizens' Rights

Although the rights of Canadian citizens have existed for many years, laws have not always been in place to enforce those rights. Passed in 1982, the Charter of Rights and Freedoms is part of the **Constitution**, the supreme law of the land. The Charter guarantees the rights of all people living in Canada and describes the specific rights of Canadian citizens. Before the Charter of Rights and Freedoms was enacted, the government could limit rights and freedoms at its choosing. Canada is now a constitutional democracy, in which the government has less power to deny rights and freedoms to its citizens.

Queen Elizabeth II signed the Constitution Act on April 17, 1982. The Constitution Act includes the Charter of Rights and Freedoms.

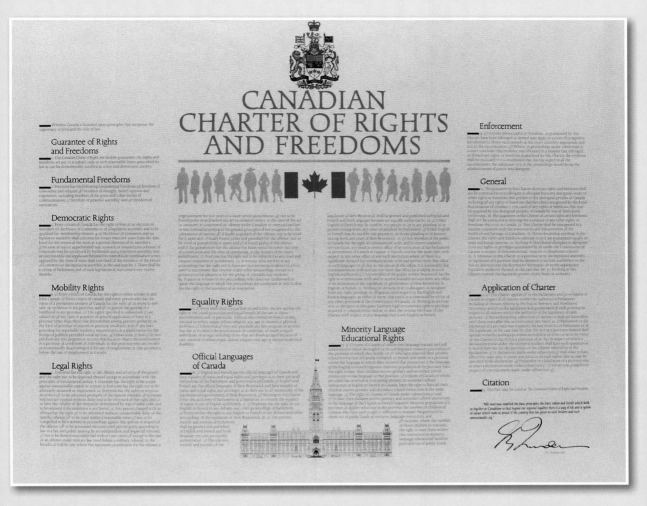

The Canadian Charter of Rights and Freedoms

Adding the Charter of Rights and Freedoms to the Constitution was an important step. People's rights are much easier to protect when they are written laws rather than customs or traditions.

The Canadian Charter of Rights and Freedoms defines the rights Canadian laws will protect. People who believe their freedoms have been violated have the right to seek protection. Likewise, citizens who see unfair treatment of others have a responsibility to see that the rights of those people are protected.

The Charter helps balance government power and individual freedom. Government cannot violate the rights and freedoms of Canadians. Citizens who believe their rights have been denied can seek protection from a court of law. The courts have the final say regarding the scope of Canadians' rights.

The Charter of Rights and Freedoms bears the signature of former Prime Minister Pierre Trudeau.

The Charter of Rights and Freedoms

The Charter gives people the right to practise any religion. Sikhism is one of the many religions found in Canada.

The Charter of Rights and Freedoms outlines Canadians' fundamental freedoms and a number of specific rights. The Charter addresses five groups of rights. These are democratic rights, mobility rights, legal rights, equality rights, and language rights. Some of these rights apply only to citizens, while others apply to everyone living in Canada. Understanding the Charter and what it means to Canadians is essential to the idea of citizenship.

Guarantee of Rights and Freedoms

Section 1 guarantees the rights and freedoms listed in the Charter. It allows the government to pass laws to limit freedoms only if those limits are reasonable and justifiable in a court of law. This section creates a balance between citizens' rights and freedoms and the good of society as a whole.

The Charter guarantees the freedoms of expression and peaceful assembly. This allows people to hold peaceful public protests.

Fundamental Freedoms

Section 2 of the Charter outlines the basic freedoms that all citizens are guaranteed. These are freedom of conscience and religion, freedom of thought, belief, opinion, and expression, freedom of peaceful assembly, freedom of association, and freedom of the press and media.

The freedom of the press is another important right in the Charter.

Democratic Rights

Section 3 gives citizens the right to vote and to seek public office. Section 4 places five-year limits, except during war, on the time between elections for the House of Commons or any provincial legislature. During times of war, the federal government must get a two-thirds **majority** vote in the House of Commons to extend its term. Section 5 states that **Parliament** and the legislatures of the provinces and territories must meet at least once every 12 months.

Mobility Rights

Canadian citizens are free to enter, leave, and move around Canada as they wish. Section 6 of the Charter guarantees all citizens equal access to services in all provinces and territories.

More Rights and Freedoms

Legal Rights

The Charter outlines the legal rights of citizens. Section 7 guarantees life, liberty, and the security of person. Sections 8 through 14 set down citizens' rights with respect to arrest, searches, imprisonment, legal counsel, trials, and some court procedures.

Equality Rights

In the past, women and some **minority** groups were not treated equally under the law. Section 15 of the Charter states that all citizens are equal with respect to the law. All citizens are to be given equal protection by the law, regardless of race, ethnic or national origin, colour, religion, gender, age, or mental or physical disability.

All people are equal under the law, no matter what their race, colour, gender, or disability.

Official Languages of Canada

Language rights are addressed in Sections 16 through 23. The Charter makes English and French the official languages of Canada and gives them equal status in all federal institutions, including the Parliament of Canada. French and English are also established as the official languages of New Brunswick with equal status. Citizens may obtain all federal government services, and all services of the New Brunswick government, in either English or French. Furthermore, citizens have the right to use either English or French in federal courts.

Some traffic signs in Canada are written in French and in English.

Enforcement

Section 24 of the Charter ensures that the rights and freedoms of citizens will be enforced by the courts.

General

Section 25 states that nothing in the Charter will lessen existing rights of Aboriginal Peoples in Canada. Section 26 recognizes that there may be other rights and freedoms not listed in the Charter. Section 27 states that the Charter will be applied so as to enhance the multicultural nature of Canada. Section 28 states that the rights and freedoms in the Charter are guaranteed equally to male and female persons.

The Charter protects First Nations members and all other Aboriginal Peoples.

Application of Charter

Two of the last sections state where and to whom the Charter applies. Parliament and the provincial legislatures are given some power to limit the legal rights, equality rights, and fundamental freedoms of citizens.

Citizens' Responsibilities

Citizens have a responsibility to protect the natural beauty of Canada's environment.

Canadians have many rights, but they also have responsibilities, or duties, they are obliged to perform. Some responsibilities are clearly stated in laws. Others are expressed indirectly, or they are implied. As part of the oath of citizenship, a new Canadian promises to "fulfill my duties as a Canadian citizen." These duties include being loyal to Canada, obeying its laws, and respecting the rights of others.

The government has the authority to make laws as long as these laws do not interfere with people's rights. Citizens have a responsibility to respect the government's authority to make laws. They also have the duty to observe those laws. Citizens also have a responsibility to serve on a jury when called to do so.

All Canadians have a right to equal access to economic benefits and public services provided by the government. With that right comes the legal responsibility to pay taxes.

Citizens also have the responsibility to protect Canada's heritage, environment, and ideals. Many people choose to defend the country by joining the Canadian Armed Forces. The men and women of the armed forces are sometimes asked to fight in foreign wars to defend the rights and freedoms of both Canadians and people in other countries.

Citizens who are selected to serve on a jury have a responsibility to listen closely to the facts and make a fair judgment.

Canadian troops have a duty to protect the country during times of war.

What It Means to Be a Canadian Citizen

Only Canadian citizens have the right to carry a Canadian passport.

Citizenship gives Canadians full rights to participate in and contribute to Canadian life. Non-citizens living in Canada have the same legal rights and the same responsibility to obey the law that Canadian citizens do. Yet, only citizens enjoy the right to take part in the democratic process. A non-citizen cannot vote in Canadian elections or run for political office. Only a citizen may hold certain government jobs.

People born in Canada are natural citizens. Their birth certificate proves their citizenship. People born in another country who choose to become citizens of Canada are naturalized citizens. Both natural and naturalized citizens have the same rights, privileges, and responsibilities.

Some people have plural citizenship, which means they are citizens of more than one country. For example, if American parents are working in Canada when their child is born, their son or daughter has dual citizenship. The government of Canada allows people to keep their Canadian citizenship even if they are granted citizenship in another country. Except in unusual circumstances, people who are born in Canada or become citizens of Canada remain Canadian citizens for the rest of their lives.

Hockey legend Wayne Gretzky has dual citizenship. He was born and raised in Brantford, Ontario, but he is also a citizen of the United States. His wife is American actress Janet Jones.

Comedian Jim Carrey is a dual citizen. He grew up in Ontario, but he moved to Los Angeles to pursue a career in entertainment.

The Path to Citizenship

Naturalization is the process in which a person who comes to Canada to live permanently receives the rights, status, and privileges of Canadian citizenship. A non-citizen who has been given permission to live and work in Canada for an extended period is called a landed immigrant or permanent resident.

Permanent residents must meet certain requirements to apply for and be granted citizenship. They must be 18 years of age or older and be lawfully admitted as a permanent resident of Canada. They are required to have lived in Canada for at least three of the four years immediately before their application for citizenship. Applicants cannot pose a threat to the security of Canada. They cannot be on probation, on parole, or in prison. People convicted of an **indictable offence** within the past three years are not allowed to apply for citizenship.

Immigrants from all over the world have contributed to Canadian culture. Toronto has one of the largest Chinatown sections in North America.

A permanent resident applies for citizenship by completing and mailing an application to Citizenship and Immigration Canada. The applicant arranges for an interview, or hearing, with a citizenship judge. If the applicant is between 18 and 54 years old, he or she must take a citizenship test. The test evaluates the applicant's understanding of the rights and responsibilities of Canadian citizens. It also measures his or her knowledge of Canadian history, geography, and politics. Finally, the applicant must demonstrate the ability to speak and understand either English or French. The citizenship judge then decides whether the applicant meets the requirements for citizenship.

After a successful hearing, the applicant attends a citizenship ceremony. This special event is presided over by a judge. During the ceremony, the applicants swear the oath of citizenship. New Canadian citizens receive a certificate that proves their citizenship.

Oath of Canadian Citizenship

At the citizenship ceremony, applicants say the oath of citizenship.

"I swear (or affirm) that I will be faithful and bear true allegiance to Her Majesty Queen Elizabeth the Second, Queen of Canada, Her Heirs and Successors, and that I will faithfully observe the laws of Canada and fulfill my duties as a Canadian citizen."

Participating in the Political Process

Participation lies at the heart of Canadian citizenship and democracy. Some people choose to participate by becoming directly involved in the political process. They may do this by joining a **political party**, campaigning for a candidate in an election, or running for office. Citizens who are 18 years of age or older are allowed to be candidates in federal, provincial, and municipal elections.

Not all people have the time or interest to join a political party or run for office. Voting, however, is a significant way for citizens to participate in politics. The right to vote is guaranteed by the Charter of Rights and Freedoms.

Voting in federal and provincial elections is both an important right and a responsibility.

Like many of the most important rights, voting carries responsibility. People have a duty to be involved in choosing the people who make laws and who decide how government affects society. Voters must also make an effort to learn about issues and candidates. Being informed helps them make good decisions on election day.

Many people do not exercise their right to vote. Some people do not vote because they believe their single vote will not make a difference. No one can predict the outcome of an election, however. Sometimes, a candidate wins an election by only a few votes.

Many people get involved in politics by campaigning for a candidate in an upcoming election.

Other Ways to Get Involved

I t is not always easy for people to see how political issues affect their daily lives. One of the tasks of active citizenship is to read newspaper articles and watch the news on television. Responsible citizens note the kinds of issues being discussed and think of ways to add to the discussion or resolve the issue. By learning about the issues, citizens often find that many of them directly affect their lives in some way.

Becoming involved in the community can be as simple as helping an elderly person in the neighbourhood.

Voting and running for office are important ways for Canadians to participate, but citizens can get involved in other ways. Community involvement typically consists of volunteering in groups or organizations that help improve life for people in the neighbourhood or community. For example, a citizen can serve on a local school **council** or join a community association. Students may choose to volunteer at a food bank or other charity or tutor another student. People may also help protect the environment by cleaning up a local park. Volunteering is a great way to gain important skills and meet new people.

Decision-making is another main part of citizenship. Citizens make individual and group decisions about how they want to live. These decisions can affect society as a whole. For example, a citizen who votes in an election is making a decision about the direction of government. When a citizen builds a compost heap in her backyard, she is making a decision about waste removal in the area. Citizens might not make a conscious choice to affect society, but their daily decisions do have an impact on the larger picture.

Citizens can influence political decision-making by signing petitions, writing letters to editors, politicians, and public officials, and taking part in peaceful demonstrations or protests. The more input politicians and government officials receive from people, the better is the chance that the public's ideas will be adopted and reflected in laws and policies.

Citizens can help influence the political process by signing petitions for causes that are important to them.

Citizens can stay informed about the world around them by reading a newspaper.

Lobbying

Groups that work to improve the rights of Aboriginal Peoples are among the many lobbying groups in Canada. Former National Chief of the Assembly of First Nations Phil Fontaine (second from right) met with Prime Minister Stephen Harper in 2008 to discuss First Nations' issues.

When groups of citizens try to influence government decisions, their activity is described as **lobbying**. Lobbying groups, or pressure groups, work to promote certain causes and to make government policy reflect their own specific interests. Lobbying groups exist for almost every kind of special interest group in Canadian society. There are labour unions, environmental groups, business and professional associations, agricultural groups, and cultural groups.

Lobbying groups play an important role in the decisions governments make by getting their message across to both the government and the public. If the government believes the majority of Canadians feel a certain way about an issue, it will usually try to make a decision that pleases the majority.

Pressure groups use a number of tactics to reach their goals. Their lobbying is often aimed at elected officials. Lobbying may include offering support in the next election or threatening to withdraw support. Pressure groups organize letter-writing campaigns and hold public education events. Many lobbying groups in Canada regularly make formal presentations to the government.

Many pressure groups rely on the media to win public support for their views. They use advertising and press conferences to inform the public and pressure the government. Groups sometimes use **strikes** to protest against government policies or legislation. People also use strikes to win better wages or working conditions. Pressure groups may organize a boycott, or ask consumers not to buy certain products or shop at certain stores.

Members of labour unions sometimes stage protests to try to save jobs from being cut or to gain better working conditions.

Facts to Know

Mapping Canadian Immigrants

From 2001 to 2006, nearly 70 percent of immigrants to Canada settled in Montreal, Toronto, or Vancouver and in the surrounding metropolitan areas of these cities. A 2005 Statistics Canada study found that 31.8 percent of people who immigrate to Canada do so for a better quality of life. Improved potential for their family's future was the second-biggest reason, at 17.5 percent. Other people emigrate for political reasons. The same study found that 81 percent of immigrants surveyed planned to stay in Canada permanently.

* Source: Statistics Canada, Census of Population, 2006.

Percentages do not add up to 100 because of rounding.

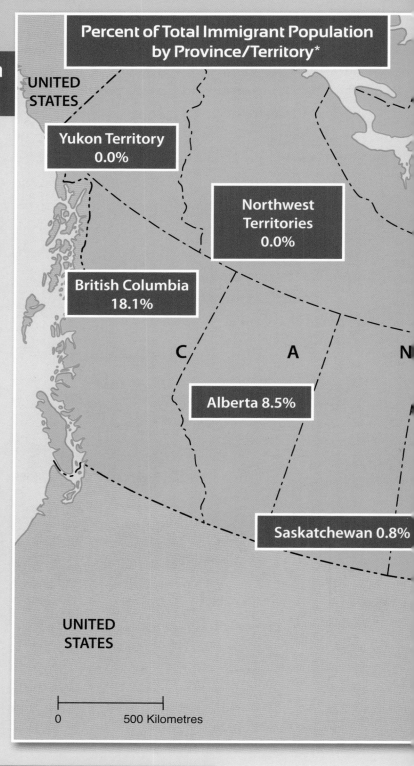

Percent of Total Immigrant Population by Province/Territory*

UNITED STATES

Yukon Territory 0.0%

Northwest Territories 0.0%

British Columbia 18.1%

C   A   N

Alberta 8.5%

Saskatchewan 0.8%

UNITED STATES

0   500 Kilometres

Top Places of Birth of Immigrants to Canada, 2001 to 2006

155,105	People's Republic of China
129,140	India
77,880	Philippines
57,630	Pakistan
38,770	United States of America
35,450	South Korea
28,080	Romania
27,600	Iran
25,655	United Kingdom
25,310	Colombia

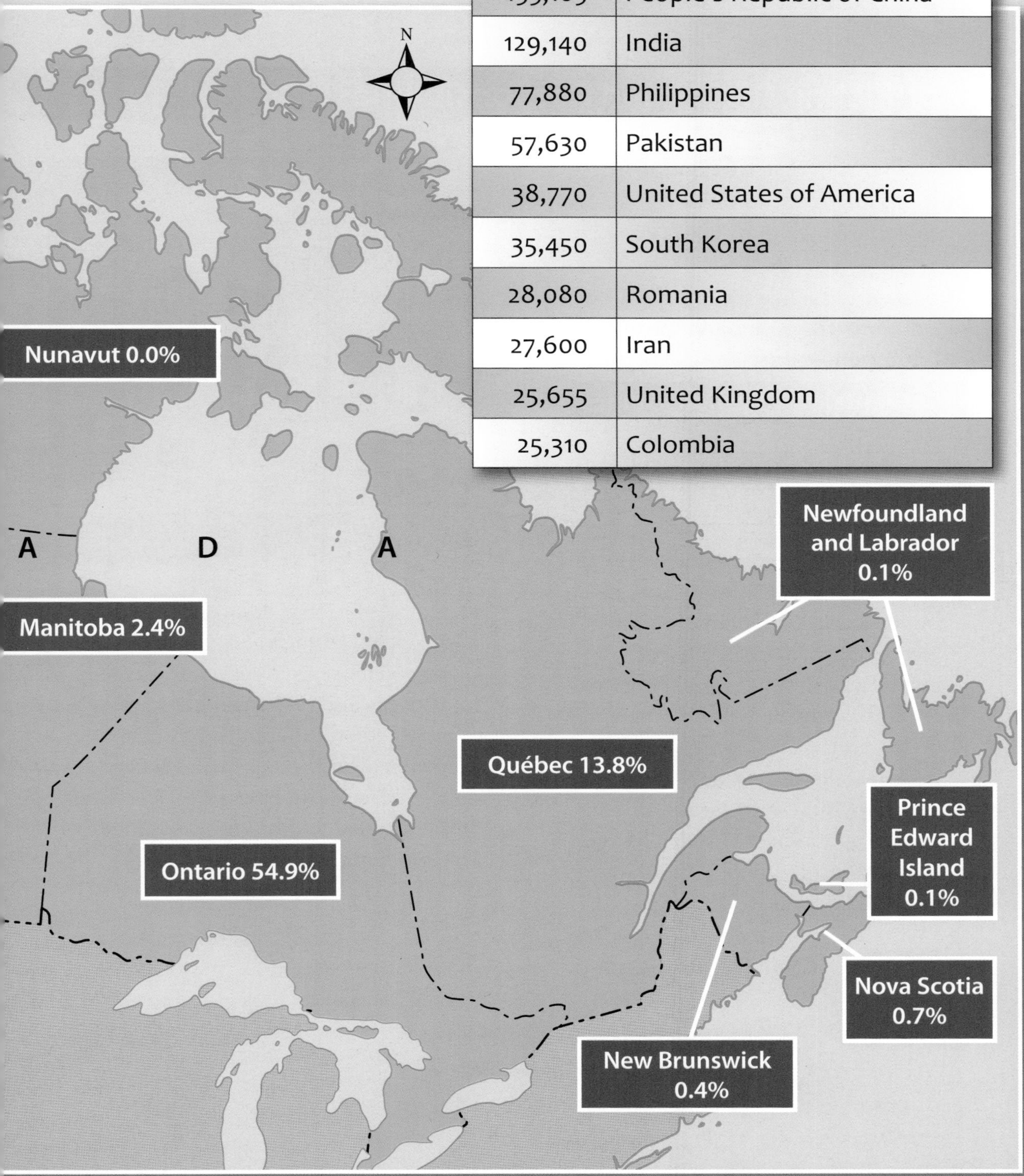

Nunavut 0.0%

A   D   A

Manitoba 2.4%

Newfoundland and Labrador 0.1%

Québec 13.8%

Prince Edward Island 0.1%

Ontario 54.9%

Nova Scotia 0.7%

New Brunswick 0.4%

Activities

Conflicting Rights and Responsibilities

Consider whether rights and responsibilities can be in conflict with each other.

1. Make a chart like the one below. One column is for rights, and the other is for responsibilities.

Rights	Responsibilities

2. In column one, list four rights that are important to Canadians.

3. In column two, make a list of responsibilities that correspond to the rights you have listed. There may be more than one corresponding responsibility for each right.

4. Discuss your completed chart with friends and family. What rights and responsibilities do they think should be added or removed? Why?

While discussing rights and responsibilities, think about the following questions.

a.) Do people interpret rights and responsibilities in different ways?

b.) If rights and responsibilities are understood differently, how can people decide on a plan of action?

c.) Is it possible for citizens to act on their rights without fulfilling their corresponding responsibilities?

d.) What are some characteristics of responsible citizenship?

The Charter of Rights and Freedoms addresses five groups of rights. Which of those groups are not represented in your list of the most important rights? Review the rights you did not include.

Conduct a Community Survey

Part of making a decision is finding out others' views. Canadian law states that only citizens who are age 18 or older are allowed to vote. Some people say this denies younger citizens a basic right of citizenship. Others disagree. They think that voting should not necessarily be extended to citizens under the age of 18.

1. Familiarize yourself with the debate surrounding the voting age.

2. Develop a questionnaire that you will use to survey the opinions of friends, classmates, students in other grades, teachers, family members, and people in the community. Your questionnaire could contain questions such as, "Should the voting age be lowered?" "Why or why not?" "What do you think the legal voting age should be?"

3. Carry out your survey. Ask at least 30 people for their opinions. Be sure to record their answers. You may want to note the age group of each respondent. For example, was the person an adolescent or an adult? You may find that people within the same age group tend to have similar opinions about the issue.

4. Summarize the information you gathered.

5. Discuss the survey results with your friends and classmates to determine majority and minority views on each aspect of the issue. Draw conclusions based on the information you gathered.

WHAT Have You LEARNED?

Answer these questions to see what you have learned about Canadians' rights and responsibilities.

1 What does the Charter of Rights and Freedoms define?

2 What is a naturalized citizen?

3 How many groups of rights does the Charter represent?

4 Which section of the Charter states that all citizens are to be given equal protection under the law?

5 How old must permanent residents be to apply for Canadian citizenship?

6 Name two rights of Canadian citizens that are not granted to permanent residents.

7 To pass the citizenship test, an applicant must be knowledgeable in what three areas?

8 Name the oath that applicants swear at the citizenship ceremony.

9 What is the name for groups of citizens who try to influence government decisions and priorities?

10 From 2001 to 2006, the largest group of immigrants to Canada came from what country?

ANSWERS: 1. *The Charter describes the specific rights of Canadian citizens and guarantees the rights of all people living in Canada.* 2. *A person born in one country who chooses to become a citizen of another country* 3. *Five: democratic rights, mobility rights, legal rights, equality rights, and language rights* 4. *The equality rights section, section 15* 5. *18 years old* 6. *The right to vote and be a candidate in Canadian elections; the right to carry a Canadian passport* 7. *The rights and responsibilities of Canadian citizens; Canadian history, geography, and politics; speaking and understanding either English or French* 8. *The Oath of Canadian Citizenship* 9. *Lobby groups or pressure groups* 10. *The People's Republic of China*

Find Out More

Many books and websites provide information on Canadians' rights and responsibilities. To learn more about rights, responsibilities, and citizenship, borrow books from the library or do research online.

BOOKS

Most libraries have computers with an online catalog. If you input a key word, you will get a list of related books in the library. Nonfiction books are arranged numerically by call number. Fiction books are organized alphabetically by the author's last name.

WEBSITES

Libraries often have online reference databases that you can access from any computer. You can also use an Internet search engine, but be sure to verify the source of the website's information. Official websites run by government agencies are usually reliable, for example. To find out more about rights and responsibilities, type key words, such as "Canadian rights and responsibilities" or "Canadian citizenship," into the search field.

Words to Know

citizenship: the state of being a Canadian citizen and participating in Canadian life at the individual, community, and societal level

constitution: the fundamental principles and rules under which a country is governed

council: elected representatives of a community

direct democracy: a form of government that gives every citizen the right to vote on every issue

governor general: a representative appointed by the British monarch to represent him or her in Canada

heritage: the details of someone's or something's history

indictable offence: an illegal action for which a person can be charged under the law and punished if found guilty

lobbying: the act of voicing opinions to lawmakers in government in order to influence their decisions

majority: more than half of a total

minority: people of a certain race, religion or ethnicity who live among a larger group of a different race, religion, or ethnicity

oath: a formal promise to fulfill a pledge

Parliament: a law-making body; Parliament in Canada is composed of the House of Commons, the Senate, and the monarchy

political party: a group of people who share similar ideas about how government should operate

representative democracy: a form of government in which citizens do not take part directly but elect representatives to pass laws and make decisions on behalf of everyone

responsibilities: obligations or duties for which a citizen is held accountable, such as serving on a jury, paying taxes, and obeying the laws

rights: freedoms that are protected by law

strikes: protests in which workers withhold services until certain demands are met

INDEX